No Time

No Time

Margaret Avison

LANCELOT PRESS
HANTSPORT, NOVA SCOTIA

The author would like to thank the editors of the following periodicals, where poems in the present volume first appeared: *Exile; New Reasoner; Canadian Woman Studies; Canadian Literature; In Celebration: Anemos: To Denise Levertov on your 60th Birthday.*

Cover conceived and designed by Karen Reczuch.

ISBN 0-88999-428-5
Published 1989

All rights reserved. No part of this book may be reproduced in any form without written permission of the publishers except brief quotations embodied in critical articles or reviews.

LANCELOT PRESS LIMITED, Hantsport, Nova Scotia
Office and production facility located on Highway No. 1, ½ mile east of Hantsport.

To my friend Joan Eichner in
appreciation of her encouragement
and editorial help.

Contents

The Jo Poems	13
I. Thank God, someone spoke plainly, but humanly	19
II. One winter-kitchen place...	20
III. Today, July 18, ...	21
IV. My friend is dead...	26
V. On the doorsill of her death...	30
VI. Daily and lifelong, Josephine...	32
VII. Pruning	34
VIII. Wheat and blue sky...	35
IX. Only all looking to the core...	36
X. Once there was a court...	37
The hid, here	39
Denatured Nature	40
Patience	41
Dark afternoon	42
Compromised — and Fighting: 1988 as through the reign of Ahab	43
Anti-War *or* That we may not Lose Loss	45
Horseless City on a Rainy Thursday	46
Cloudburst	47
"Detroit . . . Chicago . . . 8 a.m. . . . Platform 5"	48
Meditation on the Opening of the Fourth Gospel	49
Just Left *or* The night Margaret Laurence Died	50
Standing Centuries	51
Living the Shadow	53
Radical Hope	54

For Jessie MacPherson: a tribute; a portrait	55
Silent night in Canada in 1848	56
Processions. Triumph. Progress. Celebration.	58
April	59
Sparrows	60
Seeing So Little	61
Orders of Trees	62
For a Con Artist, who had given the Worker a False Address	63
For Milton Acorn	65
The Butterfly	66
All You Need Is A Screw-Driver!	67
Meeknesses	69
Night's end	70
When we hear a witness give evidence	71
Timing	72
City birds	73
My Mother's Death	75
I. The End of Chronic Care & Other Kinds of Unpersonhood	76
II. Call and Recall	77
III. Suspense	78
IV. Hospital Death	79
V. It All Runs Together *or* My sisters, O, my brothers	80
VI. Place: given	81
Known	83
In the hour	84
Winter looses winds	85
Insomnia	86
Coming Back	87
Ineradicable promise	88
Sumptuous mortality	89

Focusing	90
Riddle	91
Early morning (peopleless) park	92
Migrant impulses	93
To Someone in That Boardroom	95
In sultry weather	96
The Sussex Mews	97
People who endure	98
Conglomerate Space *or* Shop and Sup	99
When did the billboard clamour on our early motorways die down?	100
Crowd corralling	101
Going to Work	102
Withstanding	103
Walking home, Scarborough	105
Albania imagined	106
Ode to Bartok	107
Constancy	112
Future	113
Beginning Praise	114
Paraphrase of Ephesians 2:1-6	115
Levellers	116
The Fix	117
Toronto tourist tours Toronto	118
Corporate Obsolescence: a Sad Poem in a Sad Summer	119
Edging up on the writing	120
Discovery on reading a poem	121
Making senses	122
Choice	123
The Unshackling	124
Fierce, old and forest	125
The promise of particulars	126
Money needs	127
Portrait of Karen Beaumont	128
Thoughts on Maundy Thursday	129
Godspeed	130

When the subway was being built on Yonge Street	131
The Banished Endure	132
"By the waters of Babylon . . ."	133
Enduring	134
A small music on a spring morning	135
The Word	136
Prison to Fastness	137
"He himself suffered when he was tempted"	139
Beginnings	140
The cloud	141
It bothers me to date things "June the 9th"	142
The Freeing	144
Cycle	145
Our only hour	146
To a fact-facer	149
Open and Shut Case	150
Bolt from the Blue	151
The I-wants in the Way	152
To a seeking stranger	153
Noted, Foundered	155
Priorities and perspective	156
. . . the Wound	158
For bpn (circa 1965)	159
Our travels' ending	160
To Joan	161
The Cursed Fig-Tree: the form not the purpose of the parable	162
"Don't Touch the Glory"	164
The Singular	165
From Christmas Through This Today	166
Self-mirrorings	167
Oh, None of that! — a Prayer	168
Goal far and near	169
Peace and War	170

Power	171
Wrong word, because language has to be also human	172
Nothing else for it	173
Heavy-hearted Hope	174
The Touch of the Untouchable	176
Incentive	177
Loss	178
Out	179
Nostrils	180
Knowledge of Age	181
The Ecologist's Song	182
Learning Love a Little	183
Birthdays	184

THE JO POEMS
I - X

So Many Years Later:
preface

On a stormy morning, sun-tinge and tumult of cloud release the sombre earth tones of autumn trees. The last green, the grass verge, glows under that overcast.

Death looks very different when viewed from the end of life, death of contemporaries: quiet, a kind of fulfilment. I reflect, for example, on my mother — she lived 102 years and 8 months. Only this morning do I suddenly remember one of her contented adjustments — to washing her hands and face in bed: the thoroughness around the ears that her muscles remembered from the days before bath-tubs or running water, when as a young woman she enjoyed her sponge-bath. Such a subject heavy, oppressive? Surely not.

But why go on to the Jo Poem sequence? The abrupt cataclysm upon word of the untimely death of bp Nichol leaves everything altered, and so did Jo's death, for me, when we were both young still. At first comes the obsessive rehearsing of the final terrible days — everybody will have their own equivalents — and then, gradually, cherished times and occasions gleaming out three-dimensionally, not a remembering, not turning the pages of an old photograph album, but a refreshed shining out of the person clear now of time, and unforgettable.

Josephine Grimshaw (née Siggins) grew up on a small street in Toronto (off Dufferin-Davenport if you know the city) and came to university on a scholarship. We met early in our first year. When she told me the name of the "honours course" in which she was registered, I heard for the first time her characteristic laugh, a mingling of innocent delight in the absurd and sardonic awareness. "Social and Philosophical

Studies", she said, and laughed. The Depression was still unresolved by enlistments and war industries, and Jo had experienced urban poverty, indelibly. She met her husband while waitressing during a summer break, and he too was proudly "blue collar" by background and by choice, though he was a journalist as well; and Jo's choice, given her firm purpose, led through graduate studies and the bureaucracies in both Ottawa and Toronto. Her laugh supplied a running commentary on these settings, as it had on campus pretensions. At lunch-hour, during school or, later, meeting from our various jobs, Jo's eyes would dance while she regaled us with some event of her morning, or her eyes would be fixed on the others while she listened; she never looked at her plate, just groped at intervals. When a predictable spill resulted, she would laugh that same derisive-delighted laugh, putting herself in perspective as she did the stuffy old world.

We had an unplanned desolate gathering after the funeral, and one person who had worked in the civil service with Jo gave us a glimpse of her work. (I met him on that one occasion only and do not not recall his name.) He was a statistician under Jo's direction working up the data required by Ontario's Deputy Minister to support legislation on minimum wage rates for the province. Whether the outcome was the 1960 law, or the 1963 amending legislation, I do not know. Jo died in 1967.

Their section was working to an assigned deadline. Overtime was increasingly involved, and cheerfully accepted on the whole, because they all knew that any delay with the supporting documents could be used as an excuse for stalling on legislative action. One afternoon the Deputy paid a visit to their section. He and Jo conferred, and the others went on with their work. But on his way out he turned and said to Jo, now in a voice they would all hear, "I am sorry that it's earlier than the deadline we had set, but we will need your analyses tomorrow to have the time we need if we are to include the legislation in this Session."

Then, Jo's friend reports, she picked up the large glass,

government-issue ashtray from a nearby desk and as she hurled it to smash against the wall, she said, "We will have everything completed for you tomorrow." And the whole section rose and cheered, knowing it probably meant no let-up for a night and most of the day ahead. "And we made it," he said, "and so did the Legislature, in that Session."

What did Jo look like at that time? Sun-streaked, corn-coloured hair, those flashing (or dancing) blue eyes, a face agreeable in spite of a long jaw and slightly protruding front teeth — orthodontics had been out of reach when she was little. She wore her skirts long (perhaps not bothering to shorten them), and "heels", usually walking briskly with a heavy briefcase in her hand. She was thin but vigorous, and her whole bearing was resolute.

The valour of her public service I wish I could properly celebrate — her field (labour economics) is foreign territory to me. The sunniness of her friendships, with all sorts of us, I do know; and her joy in their rambunctious dog Frodo; and her stubborn persistence with piano lessons as a beginner in her thirties; her equanimity in icy flats during low-income periods or in the comfortable house they later owned, and their hospitality, I remember; and the family's support for one another and their respect for their own and other people's privacy.

Why delay so long with "the Jo-poems"? At first, to give perspective, i.e., was the initial version just therapeutic writing, an effort to relieve my own grief? If not, what was the source of uneasiness every time I re-considered it? Had Jo's death uprooted a whole tangle of vegetation that only time could sort out?

In the end, that initial version, most of it, is here, tangle and all.

Full daylight among the trees and buildings outside the window now, a busy world in a new day, far out beyond the time of Jo's life here. But parallel griefs go on. And by now there seems to me something to be openly commemorated.

*Taking sides against destructiveness
brings on the very evil of destructiveness
unless it is clear that
no two persons
will or should
entirely agree,*

i.e.

one must so take sides.

I

*Thank God, somebody spoke plainly,
but humanly.*

The skills of statisticians
mastered, lead through

The knowledge of administrative law
compassed, leads through

The questionnaires, the tallying,
the scrupulous data, all lead through

to the step beyond quantity,
beyond measurables,
beyond concepts,

out where theory is
challenged by the existence
of persons

    for whom (through
statistics, law, data, wearying
detail, unwearying work)
dignity, the
structures of dignity
may yet be
        provided.

    God help us if we can't remember this.

II

One winter-kitchen place we were, glassed in, under, together:
glass-frames were painted green. The chairs were
painted. Some had curtain-
material cushions on.
The snow-light mushed across from the
              outstretched west. Family and guest, we ate
              a family meal. Then time expanded,
              time to be there.
You wore a cast and
hobbled (newly moved in).
You spoke disconsolately of the city left
behind: "maroon plush
reception halls, glazed office warrens,
savagely cold, ice-antlering, wire tangled."
The "work" was done
but it turned out to be
in-process model-of-work, instead of
honest work. (On Salem Avenue where you
grew up, Jo, awareness comes baldly.)

After good hours, the coffee pot
glued up the oilcloth.
Our cups went cold. Ashtrays overflowed.

III

Today, July 18, 1967,
one troubled night beyond
the time-freeze:
    Jo there, locked in, flat down,
    overwhelmed (alone) with
    waves of total pain — the
    dog shut up in the house lopes between
    the suffering and the glass-panelled
    front door, lopes, hopes to be
    helpful, is
    intent; whimpers . . . .

Husband (from work) and son
coming almost as soon as the city ambulance to the
hospital. But someone else
knew? and long, so long
they did not know.
    So many
    into Emergency, the
    waiting
    room.

A handful of nurses and record-keepers and
one or two doctors. People
sharing dimes to make their calls and
telling each his own story and
helping each other find the washrooms and
apprehensive:
('if you have your own doctor' it
'helps'). So few to help too many
hurt, to answer so
many anxious.
The youthful doctor knows two things:
his human sense of what one being feels,

even the other, the not-himself;
his range of competence, the immediate basis
for making rush decisions on
three 'cases' at once (and hundreds 'outside'
'waiting for beds').
One clouds the other; he feels he must deny
his feeling.
> For the young doctor this denial seems
> essential to keeping a social trust
> (as he works on in his own
> corner).

For Jimmy and David, at the moment,
terror polarizes (the
utter need to trust
and angry consternation when a doctor,
    seeing, denies).
(The old father on the telephone
weeping — 'I only keep praying all the time' —
to One who once shone forth
against gravecloths and clay.)

> Yet my heart chokes on earth.
> My questions choke me.
> Who could discard any who cry
> 'I can't believe' — an only mortal truth
> spoken in death's presence,
> airless in its silence.

The body of death is judged now, will not stay:
    newness will come, at one touch,
        aliveness; — but
there's worse than nothing, any other way.

> Coming to that hour
> meant choosing to endure
> these groanings, too, so choosing, rather than
> letting a grave-cloth-and-clay body be

>   no worse than simple death's, eternally —
>   if that Cup had been tossed into the grass, to lie
>   abandoned, and rabbi and friends just slipped away.

But choosing so to die
means, here, and there, through love
life for good in its full power
of resolute splendour.

Teeth set, taking that dare,
facing (among the rest) the questions we
stare at till, slowly, the old horizons
>   fill with shining, overspill:
>   faith, hope, love, are one;
>   faith is not alone.
>   One is not alone.

Word spreads. Concern
rises. Helplessness
paralyses. Here is the warm-hearted
loving well-loved friend whose
heart has been open, though
seared by disorientations, danger,
dullness, toothache, the shock of
cultures, and of denials, keeping clear
a beauty almost revealed.

At work. a green
branch and a brick
wall. A telephone-call.
Tears welling wholly for one who 'just
>   heard', quickening to
>   the too much:
'It begins to seem
as if it is unlucky, knowing *me*!'
>   (Where is the power
>   to bear, to be
>   fully released, fully
>   available?)

Myself, in the odd march
of these developments: very
practical, very
sensible, very
up and down in emotions. And
evasive, looking not quite at
their suffering, all
three of them
and her father's alone at home,
dimly aware of the
strange pressure of a Presence, of a
prince of this brute, bald,
groan-choked, clammy
time, or of all
in time and out.
Fear. Panic fear.
    'Help us
 in this thine agony
 again.'

    Lake blue through
    blowing lilacs
    deepens skybloom

    One dead Lombardy
    brooms up among
    greenness fresh-billowing
      (bottle-green ditch and
        dandelion: foreground)

    The day lifts up
    (from full-bosomed loveliness)
    our railroad sadness,
    tearless,

    from behind windowglass.

Josephine, sorely beloved of God,
that day instead of trying to
tell, I found you dying.
   Out in an almost capsized ship, the Lord
"rebuked" the storm.
The storm that swamped your life
so suddenly
somehow, surely, too, he
rebuked. Calmness
unshakable, came perhaps
when you lay still, only asked
for Frodo, that gallumphing animal
who'd led me to your bed
through the locked door
and then lay near, beseechingly,
fixing us with devoted, steady eyes
until the ambulance came.

Abraham knew by faith   obliqueness –
that the boy Isaac mattered —   implicitness –
yes, to all *three* of them —
and so could totally risk
submitting. And
all three, finally, mattered.

IV

My friend is dead.
She did much good
first in her family also in
her friendships and not least in
tough-minded steps towards
protection for the most exposed,
e.g. the night-shift dishwashers &c.
   who come and go within a week
   too ill too far forgotten
   to care that 'no work' is
   also 'the worst,' or maybe
   simply not able to recall
   which allnight spot it was
   they should be turning up tonight . . . .

She cried both 'Thank God' on
the day of the attack
when help arrived, and,
in the throes, her head
rolling, through set teeth
"O Christ, O Jesus Christ" —
as I had heard her
over our thirty-one years about this earth
together, in
uncontrollable laughter, in
anger, in
outraged impatience with
unjustness, in
all the bright patches of her
staggering sense of the absurd.

My friend is dead.
Her parents, counting on their only child
say 'Joey's — gone!' as though
she'd skipped again, as

in the black 'thirties she was 'gone' to
marry, game in the teeth
of every kind of —
   cash and in-law and
   Chapel-vs-Catholic
           opposition.

Only now we learn
why she and Jimmy so often
walked hand in hand. He
broke his foot, the day before she died,
stumbling at a curb, and
refused crutches — 'I couldn't
see far enough to
put them down safely' . . . .

   My Lord, in horrible need I
   turn to the Book, and see
   sin and death, life in thee
   only, and cannot see,
   O living Word, I cannot see to see.

   I love this friend we've lost.
   And the two-dimensional good
   that was all I knew
           apart so long from you,
   I cannot now dishonour, nor belie.

   But the truth brooks no denying.
   There is a word, are words,
   that do not lie.

My friend is dead.

   The Book speaks of a Body:
   all that we know of wisdom, art,
   insight, perception, released only by
   some marvellous touch within the cells
   of other parts — from the alerting
       head

all-seeing, hearing, knowing,
remembering, receiving.
Surely this is beyond
analogy, beyond any blunt
ending or comprehending.

A singled body died
the death most shameful,
most grisly, longdrawnout,
exposed, with
two 'other' offenders
also under the emptiness of sky.
A glory nonetheless
shepherded the lacerated clay
from beyond stone to
move and speak, on the roads,
on the shore sands, in where
we are.

My friend is dead.

Already goodness enhances memories.
A goodward life flows strongly
for all our implicit otherness.
   Can one cell be inflamed perhaps, pain-radiating
   from pinch or twist, whatever
   the Evil could devise,
   but in the body still
   active, touched to will?
Long suffering is an ongoing loving
unto health ('how long
           O Lord')?

My friend is dead.

It is hard, knowing
on beyond your heart,
so slowly, and so little,
        only that

reverence for persons is what
love, truly, can be.

    A place of wrangling roots
    moves the young to petal forth
    nitrogen-breathers on shrunk curly shores with a
    pulse other than
    our lung-cleared veins' and arteries' —

    listening, I almost hear

    The air flows, lighted and strange, through
    my nostrils, is
    my present
    but now not our
    present.

V

On the doorsill of her death, afraid,
that clear bright Saturday, I prayed
and around four there stirred
pain-brilliant joy, holy accord.
Confident in my will, I waited for
a hospital report, sure of a healthward
turn. They said.
  'Condition poor.' I soared
  away from what they said . . . .

But couldn't there have entered
her hectic solitude an
angelic poured-out joy
visible only as new tiredness?

I do not know. The lift
was real, for me.
And yet I'm not the one
to tidy up a sum as though a
life of intricate bright and dark
and the huge mystery
of loving work, evasions, tactics,
home emergencies, and
sudden sickness, and dying shut off
by the sense-dimming ice-floes
where no one could follow
that I can know —
as though this, in my friend,
or in the lives 'lost' from any 'view'
that truly knows,
as though for them some passages were not part
of the all including.

The river of Life carves out
 its uttermost channels
(here 'hardening,' there 'yielding').

YES. BUT.

These human words burst out
and will.

Daily and lifelong, Josephine,
you gave voice to the mute
hoping the deaf would hear, who all
too easily, in affluent times,
relegated the poor to a category
(the 'residual poverty' of efficient,
ah, and political, theory).
* * * * * *

Having

   Sir, you have nothing
      the woman said
   Nothing to dip into water
      or carry water in

   On the empty-handed earth
   the snow stars blot and fur and dwell
      roughing eyelashes of winter grass
      and on the open gaze touching, muffling.
   On the snow the slow, rich sun, in time
   Seeds   roots   coolness
      through a new sundeep season.

   The heart listens.

   'You have a cup
   when I have nothing.
   Both must be
   for still refreshing overflowing new-day
      joy to be.'
      * * * * * *

The tulips were cherry red.
   now splayed out they are unable to
      breathe out the light that falls on them.
      * * * * * *

Boys toss sticks
aloft where spring
lit chestnut candles. Now their swollen wicks
lack not even polishing.

Reaping is rough
on field-mice in
the bloodied stubble. Grain is enough
to garner since that only nourishes man.

Dying is fall
of leaf, or day.
A body sculptures desuetude,
outguttering. And yet, it will,
in time, know everlasting awe.

* * * * * *

sky and earth seem to strike each other.

VII   Pruning

Deciduous scented
truck basket, fragrant
branch-loppings in
full leaf, branch springing and
toppling upon branch, twigs
shedding green and wood crumbs on the
curb-line from the truck's trailing
as it starts up at a signal.

Were these branches
diseased? No.
The leaves are squeaking with juices.
Was their tree or were
their trees then
hurt? Can its (or their)
sap flow and diffuse to invisible leaves?
Some trees are trimmed
for buildings or wires, and some
for sturdiness?

Pruning. The
new air
washes in, almost
visual, with
the beautiful, bitter green.

VIII

Wheat and blue sky;
a sloping hill
golden and blue
and still:
>your colours, Jo,
>your clarity.

The sunny snow
of January
your birthday time,
bright, with winter birds
trampling the snow, tilting the limb
of puff-laden tree, and scared
by a quick laugh, a slam
of a door — away!
>your window, Jo.

There need not be, there are
no words for
what is clear.

Now our hearts gather
dear recollections
wordlessly
together.

IX

Only all looking to the core
of life's forever Fire
— no more centrifugally —
can any be.

X

Once there was a court
doomed, and a scheming
truth-anointed, cold
assassin, doomed to succeed
the by then suffocated king.*

It is told that a long look passed
between the speaker of truth and
the one who would soon be a murderer.
The anointer spoke words only
of (truthful) hope for
the victim.

But then he broke down.
The murderer, startled at this weeping,
asked 'Why?' — did he want it named
in advance? it was
focused, surely, on him?

The speaker of truth was wracked
by his people's coming suffering
under the heartlessness of the oppressor.
But he spoke, he submitted in truth
to the Purposer of
what was to be,
weeping, bowed at His knee, not suppliant but
in ever-deepening love knowing
he was not in control,
could not be, would not want to
foreknow more than he must.
He clung to love as the end and so
could honour both truth, and trust.

---

* *2 Kings 8:8ff.*

The hid, here

Big birds fly past the window
trailing string or vines
out in the big blue.

Big trees become designs
of delicate floral tracery
in golden green.

The Milky Way
end over end like a football
lobs, towards that still
unreachable elsewhere
that is hid within bud and nest-stuff and bright air
where the big birds flew
past the now waiting window.

Denatured Nature

The little toothpaste-foaming waves
have wilted one wasp on the wet sand.
Last winter's snowfence sags. The beach
is drifted with washboiler
jetsam; and tossed scraps
of paper, one old shoe, give evidence of
party strays who flitted
here, before spring.

The fussing water
wads the wasp's wool,
pulping this too but
salvaging nothing.

Patience

Still, still, the trees in morning thaw,
sealed still against steel cold
and ragged on the windward sides (the conifers)
let wilted-petal light
tip-touch every needle, the least twig,
motionless.

They are prepared
for onslaught when the obliterating
blasts sweep in again.

Meanwhile they dwell
thus, now.

And they are ready
even for spring, to swell
sing break spiral shimmer
transform,
when that becomes the
inconceivable now.

Dark afternoon

The sun is white,
snowblear all stained, and
radiostore music
parlours this grimy salt-besplattered
sidewalk.

The time is furtive, seeming late,
unfurnitured, fit for hunched
non-householders, and for ghosts of a
pre-city, one-day day.

*Compromised — and Fighting: 1988 as through
the reign of Ahab*

Building, celebrating, feasts,
selective hearing of appeals
(with many too nervous to appeal),
persons accounted for, and beasts,
a desert-locust whirr
of life: no edge, all blur.
Am I subject to Ahab? I concur?

> Whining when pushed, and left aside
> in valorous protected pride,
> indignant — while I hide.

The clover-delicate light withers. Soiled
rags of cloud smear down.
Blunt moths glue to the dingy pane.

> By one act in the clear
> I might declare
> one phase of truth
> and yet still play for truce . . . .

It rains, upon the just and the unjust:
snowsoak and sloughs of April merging
until worked furrows become slop,
a muck, where seed will rot.

Fertility cultists, note
how lush begins to bloat
with bluegreen brilliance — but nothing for food.

> Moralist. Scold. Blue ruiner.
> Begin to learn to be less rude.
> Conserve the drastic judgments for export.

Sunscald on cliffs
sunblinding
water-glitter mirage

salt scurf
sleeves of sand
sand hems, and sheets of sand
(cliff-silt, so sand-powdery) sunwhite scarfing
shifted and shell-mingled and swept
so shadow-shaled even a fly's foot skids.
Crumbs cast shadows.

Here, also, angels minister.

Anti-War or *That we may not Lose Loss*

On valleyfloors under the sea
crews of old sailing ships sidle.

Whose is the cliff-path, whose the sun-bald doorstep
signalling still, "Here he will be
no more"? Whose? — and not being sure —
makes desolate ocean's floor.

> Cities have vapourized. Somewhere in slots
> or stalls we have parked the bolts
> for the blue to sizzle the fat
> off the world, or all of it dessicate.
>
> Grieve for the bracken, the honey-combs set in the orchards,
> grieve for otter and chipmunk, and those who yet on the verge are
> trusting grown-ups for food and future,
> jumpy, weedy, clouded
> already by the foreboded,
> or unafraid and dwarfed by that.

So many losses sing
in the ears as though unsung.

> Still, steady days roof over
> Jill, Alexandra, Christopher.
> Clicketing cities speak their
> various tongues, delphineal poplars
> tremble with morning light
> or shine in evening. Every single one:
> Go on! Go on, to know
> in time even the least

blessing — to cherish in want on earth
the dignity of one significant death.

Horseless City on a Rainy Thursday

Seething and smoking, the rain breathes
earth and wet board smells, juniper-berry smells,
dog's fur; o, and the pale wet
smell of a shin stripped on the cherry bark
in a near fall. This day
dwindles us, only absurdly. See
the usual street-and-corridor range as though
a ladybug rambled along
the buggy-shaft in an old shed,
sensing around its small self
context and whole conveyance —
slant and athwart and boxed and
contrived, though horseless now —
in a remoteness, a somewhere-once, abandoned.

Watery sun
appears. Ladybug tentatively
unfolds a wing.
Still the ditched farmyard steams
here, in the almost empty shining streets
with their curbs foaming.

Cloudburst

Earth (meadows and rock
gardens, perforating cities,
crepe sea-skin, people, slag mounds,
highway access ramps)

Earth (i.e. all within the
circle of sky)

suffers, today, the rain.

> Plip plip then
> (crack!) it's boiling everywhere.

> It singles itself into
> slow droplets on car windows.
> The forehead feels its skywarm touch.

> Rainworms emerge, deep waters
> under the earth are nurtured
> and, gradually, the roving clouds again.

Earth suffers the first large splats, the rush, the pelting,
   the beautiful withdrawing,
variously receiving, mirroring, waiting
for the long wind, for evening sun.

"*Detroit . . . Chicago . . . 8 a.m. . . . Platform 5*"

We queue in long young shadows
for the 8:00 o'clock bus
to the far country.
It finally shows
up at 8:30.

One, when he delays
has good cause:
outrageous care, still hopeful promise.

Does he delay?
                the timetable is not posted.
                The depot is where each is engaged till then.

Why have we less, then, trusted
  this perfectly punctual
    perfectly considerate
      perfectly timed coming

than — at 8:27 — we still unquestioningly expected
the 8:00 a.m. bus to the far country?

*Meditation on the Opening of
the Fourth Gospel*

Un-tense-able Being: spoken
for our understanding,
speaking forth the 'natural world' —
"that," we (who are part of it)
say, "we can know."

Even in this baffling darkness
Light has kept shining?
(where? where? then are we blind?).
But Truth is radiantly here,
Being, giving us to Become:
       a new unfathomable genesis.

Come? in flesh and blood?
Seen? as another part
of the 'natural world' his word
flung open, for the maybe imperiller,
in what to us was the
Beginning?

The unknown, the unrecognized, the
invisibly glorious
hid in our reality
till the truly real
lays all bare.
The unresisting,
then, most, speaks
love. We fear
that most.

Just Left or *The Night Margaret Laurence Died*

Bare branches studded once with jewelled birds
Someone inexorably plunders
One by one till an
Impoverished wintry sky from hill to
Darkening hill reveals
Untreasured tree-spikes, almost only
(One bunched bird left
His eye aglimmer there).

Waiting, dim
Loneliness, place of
That withdrawing vision —
More than the well of light from
The first far planet —
Fill, fills, fills, fills.

Mutable mortal night
Blinds mortal day
Still to changelessness.

The perched, askew,
Will ruffle still as the day-ocean
Lips in and foams towards flood of
All emptiness exposed.

Standing Centuries

In remote Ur of the Chaldees
a primitive man utterly alone
is struck, a coal shedding stars
deep as space has grown.

In elegant brightness, linen and stone
finality, Egypt rose
mirage-clear under the blue when
famine was stalked by the Jew's

deep prisonrock-born eyes.
His people — near that throne
and in time slaves — by force
were (skeleton or steel) withdrawn.

Crumbling waves behind, a dune-
carved sill on nothingness
except sandstorms and silences to hone
down an arrowing purpose

fire-cruel on cluttering cities,
petal-queer on the clean
stem of the water-freshened place:
ununderstood life flowed on.

Judgment and corruption
cone up, tumble aside, release
the kingly gold and ivory, the stone
lifting its awful grease-smudge and incense.

From the shepherd-king's loins
through refugee years, mean
resignation, compromise,
essential fires burned down

to an outcast's child born
in the cot of the beasts.
(Shepherds heard silver horns

from remotely royal stars).

That life against our own
makes much make no sense.
Who doesn't hear wild John?
Yet even his repentance

won't let even him in
to unlatch the sandals of the sourceman.
"Not worthy" he says. He can
only wait till that one

himself comes, puts on
the towel, looses the sandal thongs,
kneeling. He began,

being of the Alone,
the singing that, from the farthest down,
lingers and will resound.

Living the Shadow

Having just caught, past its foul hinder-
parts, a connecting bus — unkinder,
caught by the next bus in its splash, with glower
I make it at the appointed early hour:

doors locked, lights out still. It is clear
one of us got it wrong. Me? or the other?

Then at a word, the usual skies
open till my heart,
joyously piping, sees.

'Rising early, sending' (this, 'He saith').

No mistake. He, often even, saw
where I was — and was not — and why.
The glory of Beyond-Beginnings would stoop
to let *me* stand *him* up?

O yes! Cipher as slowly as I may,
this missed appointment's made my day.

Radical Hope

The blessing *(la blessure)* of growth
given in the broken Root,
           First-Fruit from death
as from the death we laboured for so long
now gives life worth.

Earth is now opened too
to astronomical warmth, to cultivation
as rain and secret earthworm tunnellings
prepare the way,

thawing now root-force,
proving that strange power
hid in a seed for growth.

For Jessie MacPherson:
a tribute; a portrait

A welling-up out of the earth
as brownly twilight brings on
night in the prairies,
surround of richly human pain:
not your own, not
ours, not —
even in the bedrock you insisted on —
known or discoverable . . .

That slow horizon-wide
curve, that engulphing
caused austere excellence to so
deliberately *soar:*
music — as only rises from
such silences.

Silent night in Canada in 1848

The night, a winter moon's, was, distinctively
still.
The farmers near the gorge
heard it emerge
large and unreal, and lit their lamps to pull
on boots and sheepskins and go look.
They saw Niagara-no-Falls: moony rock
with here and there a slack
curbed puddle in the moonshine,
table-paving and threshold of cataract
as actual, still, stone.

In England tallow snowlight fingers
warmed branches on the hedge;
here a son, there a husband
(among the Sikhs, some, some fighting the Trekkers
between the Orange and the Vaal)
are a broad earth-curve far from home.

Erie is wide and shallow and windswung
in a black-bushed stump-rough nowhere.
News is hard come by here
and who's to care
on the escarpment in March weather?

The moon floats round, reflecting
1848's Europe in turmoil — and
in Chile the intellectuals too
infected with revolt.

A violent gale had
jammed the ice
from Erie's floes to form
a wedged wall, locking in a vice
Niagara's sluice.

The moon floats over David Livingston,

enjungled, planning his next walk
   out across Kalihari,
over multiple campaign pennants, over
the cradle of — eyes buttoned shut in
            sleep — one Paul Gauguin.

The farmers stare at the rock, rock at the moon.

Now while it snows we linger
stunned by the roar of the Falls
and the river unrolls, unrolls.

Processions. Triumph. Progress. Celebration.

At roadside, spectators
gnaw olives, all eyes, as
the Inquisition leads its "victim" who is
also gnawing olives (old friend,
you saw, remembered, that)
before the hood was
lowered, and the rest;
sweat shone on his cheek-bones.

Next showing: a blaze of bands, then
the ominous drum-beat, shoals of parallel shins
trampling, glazed
eyes, so that children are
puzzled, distanced, prance
alongside. The elders look
locked in an odd paralysis.

We see by satellite, screened,
the war matériel crunch along
tractored, mounted on massive dollies,
peopleless, cash-cold (there, or
bunkered, along with a
"control" panel connecting
people to buttons to the matériel to
death, not as usual).

Celebration? That
waits for the end of war,
and not by winning "ours"
and leaving "theirs" to be
resumed in time. All, we and they
together, gather
this once, holding our breath,
awed, watching,
          waiting, all
spectators, all participants
        at last.

April

Dark like a handful of cool gray silk.
Clocks strike the hour. Out in the clear-gleaming sky
a robin's song, silence unravelling.

The trees with tremulous-aching fingers
shaping the quiet airflow.

Sick-faint dark
limp in the arms of the infinite.

Sparrows

Do tiny ruins, glimpsed triangles of parquet,
tempt stopover, or the shepherd's purse a-wag
or skeletal milk-weed? The frail millions
flit hither
blown like the wrack of hurricanes
along the barrel-ribs of sky.
Some will be off again
to tundra summer and the chill
promise of it and of death.

No bird-memorial commemorates
the prince of sparrows, in this their park
although our king in bronze
is here. The sparrows
in suet season, and through
carbon monoxide summer till
autumn's enlarged outdoors,
quick in their public middle age
keep hidden delicate and final things.

Only whiskered cats and the
hidden lover sees their stillness, and
the devotees of cats.

Seeing So Little

In the tents of day,
under night's canopy so
long — why
do I still not know you,
sparrow?

> hop hop
> flit swing on wire
> hop flurry in dust:
> quick take-off,
> tail-feathers snooting threat . . . .

But can you step?
In the parades of years,
burnt-orange summer,
whistling fall,
and the scouring colourless
seasons of cold,
why have I never seen you walk?
Toes yes, legs yes,
but knees?

I do not want to face the fact that
loving watching you, over
ranges of long time, I
learn so little — yet too much
to "look you up."

Orders of Trees

In France, woodlots
form tidy colonnades
with canopies, in season.

Young orchards and
Christmas-tree farms in Canada
go dwarfly grenadiering and
form columns, wheel,
for passing trains.

Farm bush is clumped, then clear
under the beech-trees, thinning
out to white pine.

Burnt-over land or
logged-out land
shows modestly harmonious proportions
of new life in one brief
lifetime.

Forests existed before us
ancient and vast.
Now we have made our planet
bare-faced.

The woodlots, orchards, farms and groves
make arithmetical comment.
Not contrite, boasting no improvement, we
nonetheless persist.

62

*For a Con Artist, who had given
    the Worker a False Address*

This morning, another con
I guess. Nobody known
that name this address.
Snow sun aflame children
fawn dogs dreambound green
leafmat under snow . . .
but nobody I know
though I am nobody to
hide from, God knows.
The wide blue
morning is alert lovely wordless
with me: waiting.

To knock next door is
neighbourly. This sunny little block
right on the cartracks feels
friendly. Here there dwell
a mother, boys, potted violet,
tortoiseshell cat. She tells
me finally about her cataracts
and how next door the woman
died months ago, and there
was nobody that name there
since, or before of course.

Walking away
into the wide of day
I wonder why
threads fray so under a
blueness and shine. My
foolishness podgy with joy
contemplates the absurd
credibility of the
shouted-by-ranges-of-angels-down-to-earth

63

reality that embraces,   enclosure/involvement
this street and her not on this street but somewhere,
indulged, a little, at least
for now.   momentary —

allowed to be — in space created by lies?

For Milton Acorn

Tufty and bristling and, yes,
covertly nest-downy in spikey branches,
for the hurt of wing or not yet
free to range.

I'm sorry, Milton.

You loudly speak for the dumb still
using words culled from
the jewel-box and the strewn
back-yard of derelict motels, etc.

Still, the
sawed-cardboard voice.

It surprised me when a long rant once
faltered into sweetness at one pink cloud in a
sad evening sky. You spoke of Shelley and
took wing then, quoting by the yard . . . .

I'm sorry, Milton. Not an apology.
Sorry, with you, that one by one awareness
arouses anger, and you get scrapped
into the safest stereotypes:
'character'; in some lingos 'poet' too.
You don't care though, snorting and seeking out
lotus-petals, white water, and bright skies.

The Butterfly *

An uproar,
a spruce-green sky, bound in iron,
the murky sea running a sulphur scum:
I saw a butterfly suddenly;
it clung between the ribs of the storm, wavering
and flung against the battering bone-wind.
I remember it, glued to the grit of that rain-strewn beach
that glowered around it, swallowed its startled design
in the larger irridescence of unstrung dark.

That wild, sour air, the miles of crouching forest, those wings,
when all-enveloping air is a
thinglass globe, swirling with storm,
tempt one to the abyss.

The butterfly's meaning, even though smashed.
Imprisoned in endless cycle? No. The meaning!
Can't we stab that one angle
into the curve of space that sweeps beyond
our farthest knowing, out into light's
place of invisibility?

---

* This is a revision, because I have learned that "moth" and "butterfly" are not interchangeable terms (as I had written them in ignorance in the earlier version), and because the "angle" seems indicated in Rom. 8:21 and Eph. 1:10.

All You Need Is A Screw-Driver!

Frustration finds no anodynes
as hours of darkness rise and fall;
the 'should have dones', the 'could have beens'
have me in thrall.

Sleepless? from creativity
in me the spoiler. (Ah, when corn,
wine, creatures, suns, all came to be,
seventh-day Joy was born.)

> A diagram a plastic sac
> of bolts and screws and little pegs
> a box of sides and front and back
> and, yes, four legs.
>
> The picture all completed glows.
> You need your own tools too? just one.
> And as adrenalin now flows:
> it WILL be done.
>
> Right the first time! ? Well, 'up' is down.
> What has been joined can come asunder.
> Reverse, rescrew: the process known,
> now there's no blunder.
>
> Empty box two, spread out the plan,
> begin assembling with a song.
> With so much practice now, how can
> this one go wrong?
>
> It could. It did. 'This one' had glue
> as well as pegs and so on. Haste
> made waste: again the wrong way to,
> and bonded fast.
>
> Another day another try?
> Pervasive smell and flaking smear
> of glue — and solvent. Let it dry

and call an engineer.

Well, I am more than construct. No diagram lays out how, or can say who. Spoiler and spoiled betimes? I anyhow can yet be made anew.

Meeknesses

    An examination room, to the examiner,
        whether medical or academic,
        whether with stretcher and gowned patient or
        young scholars   flushed   intent   submissive,
    presents pathos.

The one open to alien
evaluation now is past
risking, given over
to an assessor.
        Waiting on his pronouncement
        tomorrows stand uneasily blank.
To the examiner
the pathos is his
imputed power, too.

On Peruvian plateaus or in the
mountain valleys of Irian Jaya
people with symptoms live, or die.
And wisdom there listens, fingertip sure, alert
to the bright waterfalls, and ponders
the antecedent hidden springs.

Night's end

In sleety dark
the bouquet'd trees
are held deep, under earth.

Slow flambeaux.

Green life doused still by the
pale rainswollen clouds.

Grass now watercress-green through melting ice.

Unlidded, skylit world.

When we hear a witness give evidence

Who heard the angels' song?
Those on the night-shift. Maybe
the animals. Not mother and baby,
not Joseph, innkeeper, wise men,
not the soldiers or Herod. Not Elizabeth's John.

The glory (that *once*) was clear
of those in waiting on him who now
was clothed with only our here.
Heaven knew this was the hour.
The Father gave Himself over.
A few heard the angels shine, stricken with wonder.

Joblessness now, or night-shift,
nine-to-five or in Chronic
Care waiting it out:
we like to quibble, we hear
and are faintly afraid, are sore.
No, there's no angel-song
tonight. But when someone tells it, something,
a Presence, may briefly shine
showing heaven again,
                    and open.

Timing

In pallid winter oaks
only rustled still.
Now, woodenly they bulk
leafless where all the air is flower-frilled
(lilac and almond-blossom). Why
are only oaks so black in the bright sky?
Even in spring's rich overflow
pupae are curled in clay;
the winds that straw the lovely blue
are somewhat radioactive, too.
"Earth felt the wound."* Ambiguous nature stings
our sameness eyes: her songs
somewhere, somehow, take wing.

---

* Milton, on the Fall of Man affecting nature.

City birds

Pigeons are pedestrians
chiefly, therefore becoming threatened.
Seagulls take
over in the park.
Around the bench where bird-
charity is dispensed
they squawk like highway casualties,
and rise: sky litter.

And in the November wind they,
tilting against the sullen overcast,
shine white, in a
flash, before,
stray dots, they
remotely scatter.

MY MOTHER'S DEATH
I - VI

I. The End of Chronic Care & Other Kinds of Unpersonhood

Institutionalized love
is not in the end
especially
love.

The end seems always alone.

Love was there before . . . is
person waiting.

The Epistles on slavery
mean this: I mean, service as
dead-ended in what's done.
The lovely Presence waits for
some hint, some beckoning, in
a place squared off and framed
by "principles", where
"siding with life" is a slogan.

He, waiting, is.

And those He was before, is/i.e.would be/ with,
eat out their hearts alone
waiting, some in
even-here-unfrustratable
love.

II. Call and Recall

The I AM only, here and there
and then, and now — and on —
abides. The near
light of the Lamb, there all, never goes down.

Late afternoon through the west window (closed)
beats on the beds, on immobilized
patients in Chronic Care numb in the glare.

Low sun-rays wince on face on face
in the prone populace of this
staring-eyed place.
Curtains? As inaccessible as outer space.

Silent, motionless, gone
too far to reach, each one
feels, thinks, recalls, but deep in, far far down.

Blank as scarred downtown playhouse walls
these persons cover for
remembering: curtain calls,
storms of response, appropriate — now, but there.

Long before institutional care
my grandfather grew old. We were
children spellbound in his atmosphere.

His inner-lit wondering eyes
helped convey angels; stories of Abraham
abide; memories rise
cairn after cairn over the years: the I AM
defined by stones in time.

That inner light of the Lamb
is near still, even here.

III. Suspense

Age is the belfry.
Tongue of the bell my heart.
Wind wakens rumours* but
an unweighted rope still swings
and shivers only, earthward.
Wide is the light.
Darkness too may waken
the clangour, sounding out
through the circles of heaven,
    but not where hearing here
    is stunned in final deafness.

*The "rumours" deepen breathing:
of summer grasses, straw hats,
wild roses, rain-wet
  boards of the corncrib threshold,
and grandfather's sweet linen...

IV. Hospital Death

Dark. All alone and dying,
two hours, and no-one there.
But the flags of dawn were flying.
The chandeliers of prayer
seem sure behind cold temples or
the cavernous mouth even.

It is remote — that heaven
comforters evoke,
but your last sleep is given
to One I know awake.

V. *It All Runs Together* or *My sisters, O, my brothers*
    (thoughts on the days following news
    of yet another mine disaster
    in South Africa)

"The vital signs are good."
I didn't want to leave.
Before daybreak you died
while I slept on, and live.

        How clear and bright, that day!
        Everything echoed, rang; then
        the viewless orchestra
        stopped at the tapped baton.

Leaving you, then, alone,
you only minded, then,
if touch then had not gone
for good. I tease my brain
for sense to this distress.
Wanting to hold your life
to the last ebb? and yes,
share, where none can who live?

        Rock thin soil grass mat
        cement an old machine
        walls doors cages and gate
        constitute the Between

        for pithead families here.
        (Rescue teams go below.)
        Grip, heart, upon like fear
        with theirs, and weep, and know.

The one I left, those these await
and cannot see:
they, now, are open-eyed with night, to us
unknown, radically.

VI. Place: given

Snowcrusts and crystals
outside the glass
make snowcaulked skylight of
the hothouse roof, suncold
and bright out there, pastelled
in here with the sepia smell of
peatmoss, and small sepalled
living things misted and nesting.
>   Waterpipe sounds.
>   Far thud of pot on boards.
>   Tinkle of icemelt there beyond.

(Lingering too long? . . .)

Back at the entrydoor and shed,
outside, it's night:
glimmer of farm lights, wind
whitening briefly. And
before we turn to go

we find we walk —
as though hairspun, but among
such cameo-quiet strangers —
quietly deeper
through greenhouse to where leafy
distances open out,
past trellis, orchard arches:
>   shimmering, wonderfully
>   all we'd awaited.

Not way, now — only
now.

Known

After the crash we scan
passenger lists — eyes dart
along, down, till at last we can
relax: this horror was not to the heart.

An "act of God", that tidal wave
or flood — or the lightning-bolt
that caused this crash? We have
His word, yes. He has all, controlled.

Oh, but His eyes are on
the passenger list too;
every mourning child tonight's well-known;
their dead He, nearest, knew.
In charge — and letting us be — but not apart:
for Him this horror is real, and to the heart.

Our horizons stop at those we know
so we can bear it;
His, not at what we know,
compassing our sheer-edge-of-nothing panic
and more; He though in peace and power, knows pain
for time and space, Whom these cannot contain.

In the hour

In the hour of sorrow
remembering that
  still evening sky, the
  tall tall treetrunks
enlarges the place of sorrow
for breathing.

      Chill is the beauty
      of bunched seedheads on stiff stems
      touched, touched, touched
      by the light silhouetting solitary
      hedge-seasoned evening wind.

The words of this still speaking
quicken a prepared,
preparing, known,
neverseen heartland where
thankfulness is longing and
longing blessedness.

Winter looses winds

The untidy rooms of late childhood
are now ceramic seas
though living gannets cry there still,
settling, rising.

Through clean windows, twice a year,
the outer space eyes inner cupboard corners.
Once only in a week otherwise, we
water plants, dust, wash windowsills
so that these squares and rectangles of space
may, meanwhile, unobtrusively, contain
living.

Now old age comes, with
tactics to (slowly) outwit
chaos: what's on the shelf? when
was the last laundry-day?
etcetera? Or with
containment given only to
feral light and darkness
if need be, so that,
inbetween, time may be living,
unpredictably rich,
an order, even in chaos.

Insomnia

Until
dark lifts the wait
of light: the shivery
clarity of night
blooms its white
petals felt
on eyelids nostrils lips
until its springy tendrils
in knee-joints tingle.
Root threads thrust towards
the day-deep but stars
force their way in.

Coming Back

Coming back from travels
must feel like this:
elbow-room enough
where you know roughly what's
expected, for how much,
though not quite what's approved;
and where the other people
not part of a transaction
vanish into habit
like peaceable brothers three fields over
resolved into the angelus
the forefathers brought here
in a cracked frame, or like
the implausible blonde on the
service-station's red-&-yellow calendar
on the trans-Canada highway
in the long wind.

Ineradicable promise

When frost comes out of the ground
fragrant with rain and root
in softening hump and ditch,
all new, all sun-embrowned,
the is seems what it ought.

Necessity's seasonal.

The slowly yielding earth
harrow will jag, and plough welt out
till winter contours level.

Still, slowly, more and more is known
of sun, and rain.

O that the farmer heart
were served by the computer-channelled
currency-funnelled packaged and marketable
fabrications where
we scud and skulk, puzzled
by static, loosed to veer
towards lunacy,
because we know the need
but neither seed nor season.

No metaphor for cities under tillage?

O wet, wild, city-scouring March
you smell of soil and stem-wet
here (park triangle, back yard, vacant lot).

Pocket and patch it may be, but still, here
is wherewithal to receive.

Sumptuous mortality

Children's verandah in the
lowbreathed summer twilight:
'if I should die before I wake' lingers
erosive engraving

o not alone 'my soul to take'.
The sweetjuice hay of nightbreath
smothers in luxury. Who doesn't
burrow into being
deaf to not-life for [sound/aural]

sleep, a time of sleep.
A handkerchief of waiting daylight blown
in esperance: enough.

Focusing

Given is all there is and
all is
there is
given here and
who is roomy enough for all to get in all given

forgiven and forgiving and given
giving in and
being given there

all is
here

give

Riddle

How can we "give" who only all receive?
Just as we know who only first believe.

Early morning (peopleless) park

An ornament-coloured hound
prances among autumn's
quivering tassels — morning and mist
in swaths, bright-dangled, tapestry
his lissom zigzags.

The paw pads on the grass-mat
are felt, the pads, now, cushion-whispering
pressing softly and swiftly where
sungold is storied,
                         roomed down,
this rich only as touched now.

Migrant impulses

Leave this?
    as the Scandinavian tribesman
    fled from the ice, who found
    fire, and the equator — or
    failed to find, among the sleety root-
        ridges stumbling?

Swim the updraught of air dotty
as birds, mysteriously
instructed migrants?

No "as" has knowledge of
this force who
desolates and awes and strives —
    not epochal,
    not seasonal,
only: once. Now.

Winds whip the tree.

We twitter and flip
but not in the thinning branches
who have left forms known as trees
    forever. We are
        left to the aloning power
    who gathers us   now
(tossed, tossing)
        I sit in this tree.
    We twitter and flip.
The gloaming draws near.

The sky-valve lets in a
        pallor and chill,
        leaf and stem seal,
        soil is unthirsting.

And others gather.

The flocking, the high homing
in jetstream, strange ice-crudded
light-absorbed ways:

something of that we sense,
    none of it know —
    no nest, no place.

    The summer power was thriving.

Now it draws out
    to a new power, radiant,
    fearsome, for
        flight, far coursing.

To Someone in That Boardroom

Inflooding, dark swirls over
tinkertoy town, not drowning
the light where nightly cleaners clean
or, one floor higher, light
where a committee sits —

so late?
Tired to your wool sox, sir?
Eyes gritty with paper encounters?
Listen, then:

there is a throb, outside,
a hyacinth-core, impacted, under
the rolling wind and night.

In sultry weather

I wade on through the exhalation
of the other other
this morning, through the
Name only, not
floundering down.

Beyond the clamminess and this
place of unplasma'd leafage
propped on dim illth and left
in daytime's waiting-room
   there are valleys and shores
   of more or less possibility.

It is the going on (not
   storm and relief, or an escape
   to a wind-clean shore, or a warm sweetgrass knoll)
that surprises, daylong.

The other-longing is enough.

The Sussex Mews

A fawn kitten, with the eyes and eye-rims
of a hayfever victim, intervened
between plantain and back-stoop foot-scraper.
The sounding ocean of the air
blanched the far reaches of the steep green trees
to mirror an invisible surf. The wires
sang to the purple sky. And from the harness shop
came a long sigh of musty shadow.

These afternoon occurrences converged
on children, quarrelling.
The abandoned one turned his face slowly
into the first hurtling raindrops.

And an hour later, watching the welts blurring
the darkgreen windowpane, a child would stand
in timeless exile: from the sky
that served the sun as residence; from the warm
sweet breath of air by the board fence at noon.

      Supper would be like
lonely Noah's, with his sons,
but without hope!

People who endure

Some people who endure terrible things
become terrible, are
selved, yes
then thinged, lumped together, then
earthed.
Earth goes slowly
down (as Noah remembered but said water).

Raining and levelling, clear
eyes only, the unlidded only.

There is for Noah who
trusted, a rainbow:
who built, who dared the lonely deeps,
who woke,
a sun again, and sons.

Conglomerate space or *Shop and Sup*

There is a mall
under a highrise tower
that is itself a people-channel or
chute, to the mall
    (which if you saw in small
    would swirl with bubble-people
    around and up and down
    themselves a coloured globe-full
    on display plugged in).

The individual
bobbles along alone
although unusual
clusters occur; and then
the thin-din echoes with a new sinister
sound: a voice, far-hail,
hermetic (o, unrule!).

You even slot your fill
with plastic, styrofoam,
and papered picnic morsel
which, crouched on arborite and chrome,
furtively you channel to the internal
enzymes' emporium.

Yes, under almost every highrise tower
there is a mall
and still awhile
the lonely storm and sunshaft pour
immensity out there and over all.

*When did the billboard clamour on our
early motorways die down?*

The painted bus-stop pole
is not *colour*.

Behold the trees: their tender
young green
candles the purity of this May morning;
and in behind a patient
gray-auburn rack of branches, although
leafless, is today
lustrous.

Out of our boxes, powders, vats
come signals only.

Colour stills, rather.

Crowd corralling

Hard rain.
the bean-mash smell.
leaky tin-brim spill.
grass-soak:

birds clotted in big trees.
Cotton people in go-holes:

uncontrollable beautiful
sheepdogging skypower!

Going to Work

Dog is asleep on the mat.
   The glassdoor is burning
   with morning. You can
     smell fungus and fire
     out there, only to look.

Deal with
your cowlick.

River margin is apple-egg green,
the sun bowling wild past the poplars
and veering left and up aslant
forever.

Coat unbuttoned, eyes weeping,
I sail in sun.

Withstanding

No village store, no gleaning
from a wilderness leaning
off into slab and sky.
And wind and sun and the dread way
hone every body.
Miracle-tinting crazy
hope promises
sustenance — some time.

> No bread from heaven is given
> the fasting one
> who will provision
> his own.

Or follow the green way
out of the glutinous sun-moil.
A "country estate" deep under swaying
branches offers some refuge from the whirl,
fortifies those who care
to press on, briefly baffles then clears the eyes.
High altitudes shine in the thinning air
from here: we glorify
what, from there, flattens to shops and shacks
and railroad-valleys. Speeding and drifting at once
means nobody copes with the tombstone
tilt (the iron frost found
it alone, in winter alone, and shifted its ground).

> He who in all things worshipped
> always only one
> was therefore with him
> one, always.

From the necropolis follow the tour guide,
smelling sun on the camera casing, following
the striding crusader of an earlier invásion — on still
towards the manger site.

En route somehow lost from the tour
try to follow the book
where cloves and chrysanthemum fade for
"xalapan" ("sand by the water").
Plunge? for the sun?
Patience. Patience.

> Not putting his Lord to the test
> was his command
> and the evil one, to resist,
> left awhile then.

Walking home, Scarborough

Midafternoon
the sun is white
and all earth's winter wool is
bleared and stained and
radiostore music throbs
tempering sidewalk grime and roadslung spatter.
Sky tinges, dimly then suffuses
and far fresh snow upon spoiled
snow falls thickly, furring that man's eyelashes
and felting footsteps. Even tires
ease their slapdash, begin to feel their way.

Albania imagined

See the shine from tufted top here
to the pale carved distance over
(delicately, step delicately).

A town thrusts up on the steep of rock.
Every peak and cranny and nook
is lit in the small warm evening — sheer
slabs of shadow and sheets of clear
and casement secrets making the mountainside
multiple and quick and miraculous.

A bubble of music escapes into the empty
zigzag streets, it swims out, darts,
trembles, and is snatched
into the craters of the night below.

Stillness. Till, again, on the mountainside,
tenantless morning's doors swing wide.

Ode to Bartok, by Gyula Illyés*

Adapted into English by Margaret Avison
from the literal translation by Ilona Duczynska

'Jangling discords?' Yes! If you call it this, that has
such potency for us.
Yes, the splintering and smashing
glass strewn upon earth — the lash's
crack, the curses, the saw-teeth's screeching
scrape and shriek — let the violins learn this dementia,
and the singers' voices, let them learn from these;
let there be no peace,
no stained glass, perfumed ease
under the gilt and the velvet and the gargoyles
of the concert hall, no sanctuary from turmoil
while our hearts are gutted with grief and know no peace.

'Jangling discords?' Yes! If you call it this, that has
such potency for us.
For listen! there's no denying
the soul of this people, it is undying,
it lives, hear how its voice rises, cries out:
a grinding, grating, iron on stone,
misery's milling, caught up in modulation
if only through the piano's felts and hammers,

---

*Gyula Illyés' *Ode to Bartok* was written in the autumn of 1955, at a time when Hungarian literature had come under renewed pressure. After the first 'thaw' under the regime of Imre Nagy, it was now gradually being forced once more into regimentation by Ràkosi. Back in power, he personally took the lead in trying to subdue the writers and enforce 'socialist realism.' At the tenth anniversary of Bartok's death ample lip-service was paid to the composer throughout the country, while his music remained largely banned. Illyés came out with the Ode in an inconspicuous popular magazine containing the weekly entertainment programs of Budapest. The effect on the public was tremendous. A few days after publication of the issue (some 60,000) the police on the quiet cleared the stalls of copies still on hand.

An attempt has been made to echo the sound and syllabics of Illyés' poem in the English translating.

through vibrating vocal cords — a clangour
of truth, however grim;
let it be grim, if that's how it's given to man
to utter the rigors of truth,
for jangling discord alone — cacophony,
rebellion hounded, hurt,
but howling still, striving to drown
out the unholy's hellish din —
can assert
harmony!

Yes, only the shriek will do — cacophony —
not the dulcet songs however charming they be,
only the discords can dictate to fate:
let there be harmony!
order, but true order, lest the world perish.
O, if the world is not to perish
the people must be free
to speak, majestically!

Thin, wiry, dedicated musician,
stern, true artist, true Hungarian
(held, like so many of your generation
under disapprobation),
was it not deep compulsion, this creating:
that from the depth where the people's soul lay waiting,
a darkened tomb
that you alone can plumb,
that from the pit profound,
from the long echoing chambers down
this mineshaft, from this narrow throat,
you could send forth the piercing note
that rings to the outermost vault
of the ordained, geometric concert-hall,
the rounds and ranging tiers
where remote suns are hung as chandeliers?

          Who soothes my ear with saccharine strains
                    insults my grief. I walk
                       slowly, in black.
        When your own mother is the dead you mourn
          the funeral march should not be Offenbach.
         A fatherland broken, lost, who dares to play
                    its dirge, its threnody,
                       on the calliope?
               Is there hope yet for humankind?
           If we still ask that question, but our minds
                 stall, speechless from attrition,
                         O, speak for us,
                    stern artist, true musician,
        so that through all the struggle, failure, loss,
              the point of it, the will to live,
                       may still survive!

                  We claim it as our right
            as human beings, bound for eternal night,
            and adults now — to face up to it straight,
        since anyhow the pressure is too ponderous to evade:
                    if pain is nursed inside,
                 pressed under, it is only magnified
          past bearing. Once we could? We can no longer
           cover our eyes, our ears; the winds blow stronger,
                       to hurricane force.
      We cannot hide from it now, nor hinder tomorrow's curse:
                 'Could you do nothing? why
                       were you no use?'

                But you do not despise us, you revere
              our common nature, treat us as your peer
              when you lay bare all that to you is plain:
            the good, the vile, the saving act, the sin —
                    as you respect our stature
                       you grant us stature.
                     This reaches us at last,

                this is our best
       solace — how different from the rest! —
            human, nothing fake —
this grapples with us, concedes what is at stake
        and gives us, not just responsibility,
    but strength with it, to withstand destiny's
          ultimate stroke, to bear
               even despair.

      Thank you, thank you for this;
    thank you for strength that can resist
         even the darkest, worst.
Here at last at rock-bottom, man can stand firm.
Here, the exemplar of the few who seem
burdened for all mankind, gives utterance
  to anguish, knows an intolerable duty
to say the intolerable, and thus resolve it
             in beauty
This is the true response of the great soul,
art's answer to existence, making us whole
    though it cost the torment of hell.

    We have lived through such things —
         unutterable things —
    only Picasso's women with two noses
      and blue, six-footed horses
        can, soundless, scream
  or whinny in their nightmare galloping
what we, just human creatures, here, have known.
No one can understand who has not borne it.
  Unutterable things — thought cannot form it,
or speech reach down so far, eternally, utterly down,
    nothing but music, music like yours,
  Bartok, and yours, Kodály. Music can pierce
this night, your music, music expansive and fierce
with the heat from the heart of the mineshaft. Music endures
      in visions of things to come

when people will sing once more — music, the song
of this people, risen, reborn,
so liberating our souls that the very walls
of the prisons and camps are torn down,
so fervent in iconoclastic prayer
for our salvation, now, and here,
in sacrifice so savage, so insane
to salve us that our wounds are stanched.
To listen and comprehend is to be exalted, entranced
with wonder; our souls are hurled
out of the shadows into a brighter world
of music, of music.

Work, work, good physician, who will not lull us to sleep,
whose healing fingers of song
touching our souls and probing deep
find what is wrong.
How blessed is this cure, how searchingly profound!
We are made whole
when the tempests of pain that batter and throng
in our mute, locked hearts
breaking over you wholly somehow, and sweeping along
the cords of your mightier heart,
issue in song.

Constancy

"Things change," said someone once
when discomposed to meet
a 'ghost' who called (the pounce
too sudden to defeat).

The ought-to's multiply
and want-to's get blurred in;
harder to justify
they can become uncertain.

Then the have-to's will mean
pressures on the unchanged.
The claims that intervene
no open choice arranged.

Well, intervene they do
like time which makes its haul
without regard. And who
but wants, each in his turn, that large unchangeable?

Future

Yes, the light is pale this day:
lake-light lost in pallor,
buildings without shadow
in watery morning light.
But one triangle of grass leaps out,
vividly green, so that the
silver and saffron and cinnamon
branches, sky-root-spreading,
wait, under the morning.
Had we not seen a springtime
could we imagine leafing?
the surf of wind along the summer treetops?

Patience towards the unknown
sea-light makes only us human
creatures oddly nervous, even where there
breathes an early green, and bulb-spikes show
by the south wall.

Under incomprehension, awe, nothing we can
account for, we nonetheless know
a forceful current:
joy inexpressible.

Beginning Praise

In Thee
that "white as snow"
is, also, now, become the seed
of unimaginable, recorded, good.

I (in mankind) so stayed, must stop
in this appointed dynamo of hope.

Paraphrase of Ephesians 2:1-6 ✓

Us, the walking dead,
he has made alive;
by the Saviour, God
lifts us in his love.

Once we stirred instead
at the rebel's prod,
hungry, overfed,
hunting, hunted, bored.

Now His power is here —
though awhile our earth
thrives from holy fear:
the real utters forth.

Levellers

This scarred paved lot has
people places, fifty in all;
white paint defines each of the
paid rectangles.

From here to glossy shopping
is as sewer to penthouse,
set sideways.

O city, city, here and everywhere,
things function to confuse all place,
to dispose — "mark" or "colleague."

Persons can be tricked
to act, though other-wise, to
purpose at least alternate
distorting. Mark and colleague
occupy people places too,
with or without white-paint-assigned
(paid for) provision.

When there is no more call for ruth
either one may be known, as
both.

The Fix

Trees with their toes in
water, spectral, spines
up into watery skies: they still
their air.
             Sorrowful,
those who have let water
be, without run-off, waver,
taken by surprise by earth's slow tilt
until the low land, filled,
stands here, as if at a confusing distance.
Apple-sound evidence
speaks of large plans — hill,
hidden ravine, littoral
and inner continent; and world
in its starred ball-bearings, oiled
with light; the energy is clean and
never uncertain
about limits.
            Old age,
rooted in new swamp
sifts the uncertain twilight. Wan sedge
wavers towards the horizon.

Toronto tourist tours Toronto

These were seen today:

    the sandbox in the daycare yard;
    chickenfeathers plastered to the crate-slats and
    crates stacked on the littered walkway;
    sick smell of streetcar varnish;
    a sooted brick warehouse;
    tarpots fuming at a curb
    and the air overtop obscenely glandy like the
    Fat Woman *grande pleine*
    turning, turning away.
    A demure 'residential district'; there
    on Main St. (not so named) a
    dairybar, its girls waiting like
    Swedish loaves, and its
    windowdisplay fly-speckled;
    in a narrow unused garage
    a hand lawn mower waiting to be oiled.

The streetlights have come on.

Corporate Obsolescence: a Sad Poem in a Sad Summer

The tractor factory once
aproned in streetside grass
inspired long city blocks with
hum and bricked-in shiny glass.
It was given to tootings and
merry gliffs of steam,
and swarmed as the shifts shifted.

Now jolting past
in the bad years
from the hot streetcar windows, see:
old railroad grit, strawed weeds,
boarded up windows — some
slant-broken in to shadow.
Nobody walks along that stretch.

People live near, across and up
in streets that somehow show
too the hard times.

There they are! People.
Outside a false-bright "Bowlerama":
crammed almost on the gritty sidewalk is
some 'sidewalk-café' — furniture
(without the parasols); they hoist
tinned drinks from a Coinamatic.
How jaunty, how
almost persuasive.

The streetcar colours are as
glittering-fake as their
café's. Neither
quite gets us there.

Edging up on the writing

The fellow in the library who said
he was "researching a
poem": you just
feel he is likely no great shakes.

    How to learn, and
let shape-taking in-&-from
occur
        seeing one's
        complicity in all other
        molecular chains human and other and
        of "learning"?

The thing which to talk
as from above it (i.e. the
talker able to manoeuvre it and
other things)
    is positionally to be
    missing it

and to talk of it
as from below it, snowed by it, is
the opposite, a balancing way of
    missing it

and yet
everything helps:
charts, voyaging, waiting quietly at
home, upon occurrence.

Discovery on reading a poem

One sail
opens the wideness to me of the waters,
the largeness of the sky.

Making senses

Gray by water   fathering fallen
    gold by evening   or morning

gritty by cinder   or glass broken
    greasy by sliding   and sloping

singing by combers   silting slacking
sizzling by horseless   plastic and chrome

acrid by acres   at canal level

oakleaf smoky   at late sunlevel

sour at stoneboat   marshlily stalk
      AND
sweet by wicker   or water.

Choice

Walking
    in a rhythm like
    breathing, easy and
    mortally inescapable
into pre-sunrise
    (disappointingly) gray
    but (not disappointingly)
    past wet barley tips:

carnelian of birdsong vanishes.

Water bubbles invisibly under
    a mat of root and mantling turf.

A cold sour wind — in
    infancy, yes — but
    implicitly desolate, surf-livid,
    with the weird sting of newness
    on the wet skin, unsheathing eyes,
pours over land and around
    body as over a
    channel stone.

Far, now, steadily
farther into the cold ache, loss, submission to
walking-as-being — brief panics dart, at only
                  wilderness and oneself:
one is accepted by Nowhere as its own.

    This
    must be forgone
    for the "where"-asking, who
    is (in the convergences-suffering place still)
    dear.

The Unshackling

Locked in   in fear
that evening   where
ten were huddled   came
the eternal Lamb.

Two had seen gravecloths flat
in that emptied place.
All knew Mary had heard, had thought,
presence, voice, His.

Locked in   in fear:
"time's ebbed and we're alone:
how can we bear
the word that was life, then?"

He showed the torn
and holy flesh they knew
having come in
past door and bolt   right through.

"You, vulnerable (too),
with truth I breathe,
with My love, you can go
out (too). See, you are with

Me still.
Just as We will:
you will forgive,
receive."

The bliss was quick   and   brief.
"Then it's not *that* we feared!"
With their gladness and grief,
waiting, now, interfered.

Fierce, old and forest

Cold in the lead-broken sunset
waits the sandstrip
its pallor steady
in telescoped twilight.
Wet cedar branches and wet
black moss
breathe and stiffly
insects strut in sand-grass
                ritual, unfleshed
                figures of night-shore.

The promise of particulars

Foreign travel alerts
awareness, ice-sheeted, sore,
blurred. For the first-stepping child
doorway at home or shore
of remote foaming sea — all, everywhere
burns with minutiae and risk and
wonder. For the spirit released,
too, all is
vivid, nothing
routine or lost to awareness,
and yet in that one-eyed
heart-whole wonder
tiny particulars will be
known within wholeness.
The late sun, spoking under storm
against prune-coloured stormclouds to the west
halos and breathes among
the luminous leafless branchtips —
ivory, lilac, saffron, bronze (the
oaks against the rusting evergreen).
The moment winks, is gone.
But everything is shaped in prospect of the
glory.

Money needs

Bread not eaten
becomes fur;
bread not eaten
grinds to dust.
Bread not eaten
in the rain,
bread not eaten, on
sunned stone,
are neither bread nor gain.

Words or doing, either, alone,
become stale bread
too long uneaten,
burdening us who gather now   to gather
bread, though all is spent.
Yet, sparrow-toed, hope comes
looking for crumbs, crumbs in the dust.

Sun-clocked priests baked fresh bread
and ate the almost stale bread.

We claim our stature all the same.
For us, through fire and air
is given life, in bread, and in
the need for bread. We will *in extremis*
escape hunger — and death.

Portrait of Karen Beaumont

   I.   The quiet shine on the
　　　　long grasses pressed by the wind.

  II.   deep blue water
　　　　sheered by the cliffs
　　　　white pines have cleft

 III.   sparkling midnight
　　　　breathing full carnation
　　　　richness, Caribbean beautiful,
　　　　crimson and midnight blue

 IV.   January brook
　　　　bubbling under ice
　　　　and bubbling forth into the
　　　　sun-bewilderness, the
　　　　out there, here.

Thoughts on Maundy Thursday

>His actions are
>whole-hearted, clear, spontaneous,
>and therefore can be
>interpreted, after, as
>purposeful too.

There are inherent beauties —
crystalline structures under microscopes*
hidden in cliffs and canyons from our glance who
pick our way along there.

As, for instance, the sudden awareness
>while that supper was being served of
>their weariness, and of how refreshing
>cool water would be for friends not just put up with
>but loved in total vulnerability:
>mustn't it have been almost
>unbearable (the separating hour had come)?
>Then it would help simply to
>take the slave's towel and basin there.

O yes, it was an "example", and a sign.
But more. The cliffs and canyons
are mine as well as the
equipped geologist's, just as for him
>more intricate structures
>are hidden still till the magnification
>comes, in glory.

Each time we fail
he sees our need and nerves himself
by telling us again
the way the Son of Man
must go.

Lord, make us vulnerable too, to love.

---

* This is a reference to Violet Anderson's photomicrographs of crystals; *see* the colour plates in *Monteregian Treasure: the Minerals of Saint-Hailaire, Quebec*, ed. J.A. Mandarino & V. Anderson (Camb.U.P., 1989).

Godspeed
for Judy and Don MacLeod

Plunging about this city
shoring up cave-ins — ravine-bank,
garden, intersection —
until that caring, that reckless willingness
again opens reality — the one sure
Steadier, and the Foundation for newness —
for others now in their turn,

responsive, curious, free,
both of you, having opted for the best
        (among so many good
           'careers', able to meet their exactions
           and earn those rewards),
have found the best to be, often,
the buffeting, the neglect,
the corrosive committee hours,
absurdities, blame, demands,
the loneliest winter skies and
snow-light, after early morning prayer-meeting
or a vigil in I.C.U.

The Spirit steadied and cleared your spirits.

Now, though we are apart,
may He keep watch on our ways,
and continue to open your vistas, for you have courage,
on Truth, and soreness, and glory.

When the subway was being built on Yonge Street

Pile-drivers whump.
           whump.
Day broke like a chunk
    of molar (i.e. brilliantly cold
               light/ or pain)
      whump.

Is this our woods and larks and lovely
world to fit our
natures lovely in?

Carfenders. mirrors. milled dimes. manhole covers.
      whump.

By noon the trucks snow-churning and grinding
    by have hooked and chained our several eyes
      and wound us up on motor resonances.
        whump—whirr
        whump—whirr.

There is one response:
move? no, remain and prove
who all can wait it out.
These gaunt machines will fall
    silent, will
        be dragged away,
        gone!

The Banished Endure

A contour map misses
these fine-drawn quarters —
Babylon is gristle-dry
in from its waters and
the lulling fullness of the
silenced songs of Zion.

No watery skies
show on the papiermâché maps.

The young have known no holy city.

Post stalks bald post; wired listeners
sing like mosquitoes.
                        A mighty
river of dark swirls over
bird turret, blank bricked window.

The sinister unknown
binds, leg and arm,
in nightmarish paralysis.
Only awakening would bring release,
the knowledge that there is
a knower, though unknown.

"By the waters of Babylon . . . "

Voluntarily in exile
here, among the destroyers of Jerusalem
        where we panic, indoors,
        or huddle by the wall
        hiccuping with distress, blind to all hope,
        or whirl among the whirlers
        or hack on at a root
        to keep the blinkers up against
            peripheral glares and dread,
You come, to be
unblemished, yet drawing all to
Yourself,
draining all but your ways
    into the cup you purpose to drain for good
that the pure blood-sacrifice
might be forever made
turning all else tombward
till the invisible Temple shines
promising that terrible Day
and real walls, real courts, real glory
finally, rise.

Enduring ✓

Trees wait their lifetimes
fragrantly   forthright
touching the night
and earthdeep
and my ear almost
speaks with them in the night
as I wait for the sounding
the long wind moves them to.

Tangle
risks itself in space
for contour's mysteries,
self-disclosure.

Some the sun stunts,
wind lopsides.
Love articulates the sunset-flooded
bark and arteries
deep rivers into
evening breathing.

Wooden. Yes. Cloth? —
torn in ragged mellow mornings
and sundering gales:
stark, delicate, deep-bosomed,
by turn
they wait their lifetimes.

A small music on a spring morning

Why did they put the
blue and white live
balloons out with the trash
this morning just because
the party's over — when they
thub on the cardboard still
roundly, and lift on their leashes?

Having balloons about on an
overcast morning is
celebration. O in the gray
nothing distracts from the bobbling
lightsomeness of a drift of
all-alone trembling to be touched
balloons.

The Word

Huge waterfalls in ever-travelling skies
sting us with their spray
in weeping eyes
even in our present shadow-form of day.

Prison to Fastness

We self-immured were plastic,
safe from both taint and air,
figured like truth and leafy growth
but fadelessly nowhere.

How levelly we saw it;
then we broke with keeps,
steadfast to search, no matter what,
all fars and highs and deeps.

We've burned a lot of gas and oil
and cooked on many a shore.
Whereall we've gone — and some we've seen —
long since began to blur.

The figurings of safety, growth,
have new their once appeal —
but not the plastic or the walls
< on that ironic wheel.

To tolerate dissolves when all
are tolerating too!
The galaxy shoulders into night —
what "in" there is, to go.

>   (That frozen pigeon on the ramp,
>   unnaturally defunct,
>   has come by utterance than ours
>   more signally distinct.)

Comfy as gerbils on the loose
though cage and house begin
to chill — fires out and owner gone —
we nose for discipline.

Fade the eonic furnaces?
We're people nonetheless;
no gerbil knows such monster hope
as everyman's Loch Ness.

137

Moved by the source of all that moves
the mystery stirs unseen;
in nature so long missed he is
for us no might have been.

Wheatlight on tealblue morning,
Tulips dogeared by snow,
warn us with their loveliness of
our fastness out of now.

"He himself suffered when he was tempted"
(Heb. 2:18)

Yes, yes, we say, but exempted in
holiness, he didn't (as we do)
kid himself into range to get caught in the tempter's lassoo.

He himself   not only   suffered
when he was tempted — though that a lover would
so choose to know what we know
protects and compels us somehow

but think of the roped-in, rotten,
    welted and swollen, sick,
    tempter-take-all
    maggot-ripe end of our fall:

that too he chose. That suffering
was not to know what we know but so he
could instead of us; offering
(if we will love and let be)
in place of that, his glory
in holiness shared, claiming us as his family.

Beginnings

Each of us has
some sense of God
and we're all coping
with realities in our
life.
I have trouble getting the
two together.
You do too.
Everybody does.
Paul does.
In a sense he starts there.

The cloud

The August storm
is tall as a wall.
How eerily the cosmos
unflutters like a feather
in this waiting stillness!

It bothers me to date things "June the 9th"
for A.J. Stewart (who died June the 8th)

We put the dates in brackets,
the brackets closed, complete.
How can the life we share be there
when here is still a date?

A string of hours, left over:
it bothers us to know
we use this time our hearts refuse.
Shelterless, on we go.

To the all-knowing only one
all time is bared, at once.
The lovely then, the loss (for us)
remain, both in his glance.

How can we breathe the fragrance
of basswood, when to breathe
is not our common lot now?
Sorrow runs underneath

the lucite summer beauty;
this time is out beyond
time shared; we here are frozen and
eternity is   profound.

Can he share too in mortal time
who knows it closed, complete?
He knew the jolt of time gone cold
in Bethany, and wept.

He knows the powerful lack
hour upon hour
we want to fill with caring
now put beyond our power.

Because He knows us surely
with blessing and not blame,
help (dew-minute) is manna,
our stay, our strength towards home.

The Freeing

Unclasp my heart
though that disclose all:
you have known every part,
willing no-refusal.

Unclasp my heart
from my own cramped story
to new, in-threading light, a start
towards searching out your glory.

Unclasp my heart
to, unwithholding, close
on all that you impart
till daily life ensues
timeless, as you choose.

Cycle

Fear,
      threshold of every
      prayer — a
daring, never the
familiar trust, always
trust beyond
      the known.
      Waking to risks whets;
      venturing, sparks
fresh fear.

Our only hour

In the sunslick a shrub, its buds sealed in,
is skeleton'd in light. Sand clumps on
                sand cast shadows.
Out of strange oceans day has unscrolled,
                (low shining) has smoothed
        a HERE from among
farness and blueness and more, more, mounting and melting
                to indigo, and the centripetal
                      fires of gold.
His look was lightning.
The extraordinary angel
stood, where history cleft
B.C. — A.D.:
the keepers were as dead men.

    The keepers till the day they died
    could not forget. Blindness still stabbing, from the
        fierce glare of such a
        countenance (in the undwindling moment
                when they blacked out).

    Not everybody sees
    something like that in his time.
    And then can never
    distance it by
    words ('I always remember
        the morning . . .')
    Nobody could have heard.

    Often in the night
    the old keeper would
    butt again at the wall

ของ fact: the stone,
> the hurried debriefing to
> > hide what was done
> > and keep them each alone
> > and dumb.

His look was lightning.
It is a disappointment
> to have seen
> the singular brightness and be
> only as dead men,
and then exist, later that day and on and on:
> the point of it
> searching you, idly now, somehow, in
> a gathering silence, a history
compulsively reviewed.

Could those keepers have actually
stifled the world?
One of them wondered,
waiting it out in the hours of his darkness.

> > Three women were there.
> > > God kept them from terror.
> > > Truth shone, and shines.

The shrubbery by an apartment wall is
wire-bright in the keen north sun
> > (sky jet-stream-sundered)
> > and I think
> > how it is the angel
> > staggers belief.

Wide continents, telescope-swathed marine sky, our
> Multifarious kind, spilling out, over, around:

we receive "all" easily but
glimpse something, once or twice,
which in our only hour will be
massively known.

The angel, we
hardly expect,
can hardly credit.

But the man, torn, stained,
left in mummy-wrappings,
stone under stone?

the man then seen
alive, known
powerful, heard
in the heart's ear?

> He does not so stagger belief
> as overwhelm our grieving.

To a fact-facer

When you crawled over the ice to the crest
and there was the deer the
wolves had torn
you had forbearance in the blast
    and blank of fear.

Now the candour of March is lit
and from the springing root
the liquors of life, stringbean sweet,
cry "out!"

Now, bearing this with that
you make your winter time complete.

Open and Shut Case

He came right here — and we missed him.
Emptiness swallows us down.
He let us choose to hurt him.
He died alone.

His clarity and care —
oh, we heard and saw — and
twitched ourselves away.

The goodness we want should
be exclusive, not in our power
to even say no to.

He is here now.
Anyone's heart of stone
love loves to touch to
hurt and holiness.

Bolt from the Blue

When something . . . split? — bright
terror, ear-drum-crack,
conveyed, not the daylight
beyond sky's iodined mask

but the mask's volt,
discharge within the veil
(Zeus with his bolt
they used to envisage). For all

the here, and the out there
beyond all suns shining
God is alone. His fear
is the heart's inclining.

The I-wants in the Way

Your going off alone to pray
when all the sick were brought
though all were healed till night
drew us to sleep and you to pray . . .
and then at dawn we thought
it would go on . . . . You taught instead,
and somewhere else.
      You pray
still. And we lean on what
seems "ours," a healer, not
knowing the one who heals comes if you pray,
today, or in That Day — and not
because we clamour, but
as we too, trusting, learn to pray.

Then when you pray
we are alone
as you are, not alone.

To a seeking stranger

To a man who wants life to the full,
wants absolutely. Wants. For God's sake yes:

in the milky blur of the day the Lord
has wakened me into, the long work and
the redolence the sun awakens (of
barnyard weeds, leaf smoke, snail moisture, **bare rock**)
I can forget that
stars burn, and emptiness coils among them
superbly, moiré-ebon, that you hear
always the gulpings of the night.

The sun in my sky has put out
your North Star. I go by.
You tell me.

A black storm suddenly plunges us
into a like turmoil. We both battle.
For God's sake yes.

What you asked for was
nothing but to know — enough.
Not the tiny somebody's sun
worked up like a dame's brooch to pin
cloth with.
Nothing from me certainly.
And to know yourself.

And yet
the man who lived, and died, but lives,
is judge of all the world. His
purity finishes us. And that
alive one blazons it: that he
is God — i.e.
perfect love, judging
for God's sake. Yes.

You, stranger, crushing
wax walls, honeycomb crushing
stranger, fervent for some
black, pine-cold pool, for
cleanness, and night's deeps,
in forest-savagery, obstructed
from completing that alone
being you know, and want to
know — enough:

you are game.
You know about an all-or-nothing throw.
You have told the truth thus far
to silence. Yes.

In time, farnesses
open. The bright large place
we must all need who would
be, begins to be.

The terrible, blood-guttering wood
can be everyday, too.
Yes.

Noted, Foundered

The tap of a carpenter's hammer
out on the lot.
The neighbour's tread on the tired stairs,
feeling her way, having bought
pinched loaves, waxpaper farmer's cheese, two chops,
stiffpaper sugar, wilt-paper greens, paperwet butter, and
the papers, trudging because she is hot.
These two pace the stutter and whir
of sewing-machine thought at its simple seam.

Somewhere a maiden spins in her prison in a tower.
She will endure for a hundred years but
she's licked from the start.

These are the masks of the midcontinent
where sea once moved, a seabed levelled, dried,
baked, abandoned, ours for this interim-ever.
Cities sprouted, bulged,
jostled for shine at sunset.
Rails and runways gleam and blink.

The carpenter still taps. The neighbour's aged parent
is dying in the civic hospital.

Priorities and perspective

At eye-level, abashed, I, this day
consent to think about Gethsemane.
In my hormonal youth the agony
was all I heard, and heard in terms of me.

Now a plain history is proving itself true
about Jesus's life, and not like me and you
but uniquely (still) raised from the three-day
tomb, and, still alive, keen to show us how.

No words, but on the Gospel page, no sign
of what it delegates now: his cross, and "mine,"
(he spoke of both). He sweats it out alone.
While we all huddle and slumber, it is done.

"No other way?" That's what at one point he said.
Step off the earth? that's hard — the earth he made —
why, see these very olive trees, each intricate
as is all simple being he created.

Plainly the options glared; eye level; he chose.
His struggle then would not be much like ours.
We twist away from the familiar as
stranger reality draws us, and draws us close.

To opt for wholeness God's way, by being killed
while the conundrum continues, of love felt,
though our unholy ways, on him, repelled
love and left him abandoned, to endure
so that we could be healed . . . .

o, easy to theologize this, drive
it fast across the horizon, and believe
afar, yes, marvelling and moved — above
the ground of where I am and how I live!

Nothing like those cosmic priorities comes
my way. It seems that sanity comes

from being in proportion. And this day's bright sky comes as context. To the minutest part, still energy comes.

*At Jesus's word the paralyzed man stood
and walked, forgiven, empowered.
It was for "authority given to* men" *the crowd
in awe praised God!**

---

* Matt. 9:8

. . . the Wound

Flame touched the marsh-grass,
withered harsh blades; and the flinch
of air and burning gas
smudged and leapt to a blue-lit
marsh-fire, ruddy at ground level.
Nests burn. Tough protectors' pinions
are singed and set down
crooked in the swelter.
Blue sky of August
burns with far cold fires.
Star-remote clear high
crystalline sun-thrust
spangles the tears
of marsh-island strangers
safe in their boat, safe in the river,
their water-bottle here
but their eyes smarting,
their bodies afloat as though empty
as though left desolate too.

For bpn (circa 1965)

The sign on the Library shelves tells it:

    LANGUAGE HAS BEEN MOVED.

Look.
Sure enough.

        Has been moved over?

    (Don't jam in here —
    whoever you are, here
    where Language isn't . . .)

        No.
        been moved deeply.

The park fountain is lost, lost
in the pitch-and-toss summer shower.

Our travels' ending

The sun went down just west of Utica;
lifting above the smoulder: a new moon.
The little waters in the bush
lay brown and still, although a puddle
on the mid-boulevard-grass-place mirrored
the light-washed zenith.
* * * * * *

Fish-skeletons, angel ones, shine,
or, scattered further are just
smoky simulacra.
Now with the blackening of the ground cover
a richer platinum is the,
earlier, papery, moon.
* * * * * *

Life is no longer with the living forms.
The last light, tinted, lingers
while berry and twig, distinct, out of the dark,
are etchings only.
* * * * * *

O, now the moon is pumpkin gold
over the blue and fluorescent-tube
geometry of the toll booth.
* * * * * *

A maroon tinge, low, is all
that's left of day.

To Joan

The pulpit led a prayer:
"Thank God who brought us here."

I prayed, "We couldn't come unless
Joan came by car for us:
help me tell truth in this
while praying thus."

'The power of kindness, providence, skill,
derive from Me whose power is over all.'

The act of God is found
lovely for being through my friend,
nonetheless His because
blessings, in her (through whom), also make final pause.

The Cursed Fig-Tree:
the form not the purpose of the parable *

It seemed on the surface:
'I'm hungry. Give fruit'
and, foiled, You let curses
dry up its root!

But that wasn't Your way.
Peter spoke up.
He'd heard You say
the tree's life would droop.

If it had been a curse
for desired figs failing
Your faith would be — and ours —
belied by Your 'desiring'!

For no fruit when the time
was wrong for fruit, its end?
Then? When Your time had come
but men would not respond?

Then, to teach us faith?
The mountain would remove:
our fears, resistance, earth-
bound 'life' that cost Your death.

And You highlight: forgiving
not practising spite,
and promises thriving
though still out of sight.

Might that tree help Your friends
know how you *could* vanquish
all those at whose hands
You preferred anguish?

---

* Mark 11:12-14, 19-26

They forgot when grief smote
who was King. But we see
how forgiveness and fruit
now depend on that Tree.

the tree becoming the type of Christ ?
the evolving analogy ?

"Don't Touch the Glory" *

A flower opened in the air,
its sheath an opalescence,
pure white petals, golden fair
the fragrant heart, the terrible pure
fragility its essence.

"I can do nothing of Myself" —
the Son put off all claiming.
The Father takes all Judgment off
and gives His Son His suffering, Life —
and us ("our" Father naming!).

The Spirit, Jesus's, in us
prompts, heals, suffers rejection,
breathing in stillness, dim with grace
to wake us to that loveliest face
and Holy resurrection.

A trembling flower in our air
appears all fragrantly:
each Person subject by the power
of love, and each One perfect through
total humility.

Pride is the enemy. This One
who loves, this Trinity
is giving, yielding, making known
what glory is, and what alone,
tuning our praise and joy.

The flower burns on in the heart,
fragile, timeless, pure,
timeless There, here in soil and hurt
still working out His beautiful art
of Self-effacing power.

---

*This title is borrowed from a poem I read in a borrowed periodical years ago and have not yet tracked down.

The Singular ✓

Lord let us learn from you
not to deny the glory
of God in man
and never to glory in that except one man
releases glory again
by his amen.

On this bedrock glory
the humble homestead rides where
you serve, a willing slave.
You demeaned yourself
to inglorious us
once, for that Sabbath eve
when the light died.

> Glory is One
> only, is shared
> when set aside
> to share for good
> the only singular good.

Piercing the bedrock
on the first morning then we learn
that his Amen
breathes and will shine
in time to everyman
the glory of the One.

From Christmas Through This Today

THE Light became our darkness
We rejoiced.

We found we were exposed
and were bemused.

Pointed to Light, the contrast we disliked, we
would have suppressed
the light but He rejoiced Himself to quench it
with all the worst.

Then from the tomb the terrible light
outburst
emptying all we'd gained and He
had lost.

The light that seeks us out
is as at first
But darkness now is different, only ours
by choice.

Child of our years, still help us till we know
the Lamb the only Light.

Self-mirrorings

Some few do hound and hit.
Most though protect, and will
shelter and help the hurt:
we're not bad, all in all.

> (One hit? one cries
> 'which one?' — o sore hearts then!)

In accidents and crises
of pain, passersby call
emergency services
and wait: don't we do pretty well?

> (Corporate coping shelters
> us maybe, more than them?)

Watch a child with a doll
stroke the imagined hurt,
comforting, hugging — all
care: isn't this our spirit?

> (This soothes the powerless rage
> of the real hurt
> even though then it was assuaged
> by being rocked quiet.)

YOU MEAN THAT THERE'S NO GOOD IN US AT ALL?

No, no. But that

> we're not much better than Peter was or
> naked John Mark, that night —
> nor for the fearsome next three days —
> nor through the shaken wonders afterwards.

Only the fiftieth day and the light poured
from somewhere not of us
does any good — if once

the uselessness of all the rest is glimpsed.

Oh, None of that! — *a Prayer* ✓

From the namby-pams
of the cloaking faith I wear
deliver me. From the times
peculiar persons, particular people-swarms
seem not, to me, familiar;
oh, from the namby-pams that evade
the absolute scrutiny
and evade healing, oh, deliver me.
Whatever I read or hear or see
only declares what is in me,
an ominous freight
hidden — and worse let out.
But from an omnibus
contrition, burying
the sting of shame, of naming it,
deliver.

And from the pride in having none
("I'm like that" or "leave me alone,
I'm a dog, I'll worry this bone")
deliver me.

Goal far and near

sliced clear water-wedge-shape
at sand-slope
welters as he wades.

He plunges, arrows the bright
channel between
beach, and, over there,
funnels and freight sheds and
minglings towards metamorphoses.

Swimmer becomes
bedaubed, shoves soggy crusts and
duck-feathers, chin lifted, among
prows, bricked wallfronts, iron
moorings . . .
(are there ladders? is there
          someone to let one down?)

The sun bronzes the lurching dock-glum water
as deep below footways
as the plane on take-off glints
up beyond dock-level.

Arrival is survival,
in fact, rescue.
Too remote now, he knows, that sand-spit he
so easily slipped off from.

Peace and War

A sharp-chinned boy
in the automat
tried the icecream bars
but none came back
though his coin went in.
He asked at the counter.
Said the counterman, No,
I've got bars in the freezer
but I'll not hand one over
till you pay me too.

Should the boy go away?
Who should say should?
What makes the counter man so mad?

Power

Master of his first tricycle,
peddling furiously towards the singing
lethal traffic
he — double elation — meets
his father fresh afoot from that main thoroughfare —
    to circle and
        come too? No — a palaver
in reasonable terms he mutinously
waits out, stubbed between lawn and father's foot,
all dammed-up and high voltage
with ears for where he'll go
only.
At last dad hoists him, waist under one arm
trike dangled from the other hand
and heads home.

DON'T PICK ME UP! the scarlet
struggling sobbing adventurer
wails (after the fact).

One is so powerful.
One is so small.

How can power know
not to make helplessness
what is decisive?

Wrong word, because language has to be also human

The "anger" of God?

I could not do without
some powerful yank, when I'm caught off guard in the
drift, the undertow,
the weed-mass,
the sudden hole in the shore's
rock-shelf cleft down to the
cold all-but-total dark.

"Anger" —
      our language
lacks words for what he knows
seeing us reckless of safeguards,

and knowing the beyond of 'total dark.'

Such seeing, knowing,
finally touches us

until one of us wants to
wriggle clear of some communal woe,
or misconceives response
as new-won innocence.

Then "anger" makes us tremble
once again?

But He it is whose Spirit
transfigures faith into
love-neighbour-as-self,
seeing the potential He imparted
and, oh, expectant, loving that
(drastic with everything obscuring it).

In practice, will one oneday know
how so to love and
so to know distortions and contaminants
with such for love's sake anger?

Nothing else for it

Seeing this we
fall to our knees.

We wouldn't be willing
to stop being persons
as he became willing
to stop being wholly
of light unapproachable
to become human
and die as a helpless
    animal died
    in the Jewish rite
    so that its drenching
    blood could besprinkle
    what needed cleaning.

How can we grasp it?

Being human
what can we do
but bow, and believe
now, or when glory
leaves all he made
transformed, or stricken.

Heavy-hearted Hope

Hope's not an emotion,
as *agape* is not.
It is a firm condition
established by one absolute hurt
till the encompassing joy — and that
only for walkers-not-by-sight, each one
in a deliberate devotion.

You grow by going towards?
Yes. Also: growing cells
are the most vulnerable
to cancer.

Pain comes   to see
unknowing (awe) not keeping
wild growths of what we think we know
in check. Do we replace a living
with our own fictive person?
Are we forestalling even
hope then?
O, can we err so far?

Heaviness. Fear comes too.
Chernobyl's children are
ours, too, though out of reach,
probably walking still by sight,
dying probably.

No magic banishing
of consequences comes
though they strike only some, and we
are free still.
Hope is not wish-fulfilment.

My hope, not theirs, makes me
look to You more than ever
for hope.
May Your own grieving heart
instruct my cry.

The Touch of the Untouchable

O vulnerable
one whom I hurt
sorely, who never are victim,
whose going under
to the ignorant, crude, the
victim of self-tyrannies
goes under and on and
out into that brightness
that is our hope,

your compassion
sweeps like the autumn-willow-wind
into the damps of my
dimness, with
fresh stinging rain, a breath
sky-wide clean soft blowing
with cedar sweetness,
a promise of the sharp
lapis lazuli, star-studded
autumnal night.

Incentive

One walked the roads, slept
on a boat-cushion, waited alone
in enemy country at blazing noon for
water even,
paced it out to the end
in such clear strength

that (cows of Bashan
      slaking our thirst, calling for more,
      squashing poor people and not even noticing
      and on the right days all in good order
      sailing down aisles, heaping up
      flowers on the altar etc.)
we look to him for

?no bread
no rain
leaf-shrivel and pests and
fevers and sores and
violence?

would but these bring us back to
the footpaths and open
skies among night-breathing olive trees,
back to the waiting,
the hope.

Loss

Back window with red-checked oilcloth on the sill
and orange-red geraniums the leaves wrinkley
in sunlight, root-cellar boards, a clothesline,
lower fence caving valleyward where the worn
grass and feathery vegetable plot give way to
butter-&-eggs, among some blueish
perennial sweet peas:
the place is bared. Trees are long gone,
and the clutter of children gone
and the sun washes in to the bone.

Here pain hit home.

Its home makes the plain place
invisibly surge with beauty, almost unbearable
while it is day.

Out

My friend sleeps on
a day off, using
sleep as a refuge.

Our friend works over-
time, using work
as a refuge.

I see that I have used
the holy given as
my way of refuge.

The urgent hope drove him
stumbling, once,
away, past any refuge
although towards joy.

Forgive.
Be thou
alone our refuge.

Nostrils ✓

Hay fever is a parody
of my extreme anxiety:
I fear that I may cease to
breathe. Yes. And I know
it will be so.

As a child in the forest once, I tried
to hold my breath, rehearsing so that I'd
be ready for my act;
but flesh made will retract,
and day resumed what had but briefly blacked.

Up-and-down in-and-out are passing strange
that they can make me be, oh, and can change
to immobility, rhythms' end,
as oceans tend
to surge and slack against quick air and land
though still where they're profound.

Than sense and pulses, so much more
waits, once one may explore.

Knowledge of Age

Knowledge of age
begins in winter, a thin-railed whistling gate
under sonorous pines
a few shivering paces, and so far,
from the stone house and all its hearths.

A slow slow seethe
of snow across banana branches is
illumined on a silk of sky
distinctly green, although no arch is there.
   On endless terraces of wine-stained space
   only plump cherubs play.

One afternoon bruised as November
in the triangular park nine small suede reindeer
feed on green moss. And city's heaven sunders to a
swift appropriate blue.

Summertime of other times shrivels
carbon and unmemorable now.

Anatomist, mark "alive" this bone
that racks and sings in winter's gate
under sonorous pines.

The Ecologist's Song ✓

Sometimes, where once the sky bent brown
above a creased doeskin of new earth
pillars plunge upwards, and through the thinning air
the pelting hail sweeps down.

Absorbing, glittering, the beach at noon
welters with silence. There a separate pool
has formed, plum-coloured, richer than water, cool,
shadowed by stillness in the naked sun.
A sudden gust whisks a gold shower
of stinging sand on the dark sheen.

Who brings the petals, cupped and shyly white?
Why are they bruised?
Who glassblows dew shaking the droplets out
to burn in icy leaf-tip and grass-blade
clear of the clustering wood?

Everywhere's ocean of sun, late-flowing, knows
the dark tides too, the netted shores
of land and air wrapping the lovely planet
round, and one knot of the net
loosed, one strand plucked in the net,
wake resonances through the hemispheres.

Attend. Attend.
In pool and sand and riffled waters, here is
significant witness of an event.

[handwritten annotations:]
Matt 13.47
Kingdom of heaven is like unto a net ?
Job 19.6
God hath overthrown me, and hath compassed
me with his net

Learning Love a Little

Out from the murk over
blurred lake, from smoke-snuggled skyline
high, winks a jet (dot still), man-made light
giving the sky a
petal's pallor:
our craft, we know, yet
flower-strange.

The tinted trace
down the deep sky
curdling already, alerts
skin, temples, heart, to
receivingly wait upon
the evening:

therefore in the clattering
tunnel, in the subway car
hustled, borne, we are
strangers averted, and together.
Respect seeds the unbreathable air with
  a certain dotted-Swiss, a
    scent, and one dumbly welcomes
      this, and them.

Birthdays

Brambled-in peace, sky-smoking,
wild grass, and the thick springy grass:
this is the birthday-festal
star-correlated hour and place.

There on the green the two
shapely ivory-clear sun-dimmed
children shyly come
each from far off, in wonder.

'A birthday present for me?'
Shyly the gold & ivory said:
'you first . . .' (perhaps too shy
to stir a step forward?).

'Here then' — and clay & ivory thrust
his present on the other little prince.

All the threads of the giver's
woven hidden heart
loosed (like the song of the warblers
in that place apart,

the glory of that garden)
and were all at once a bright
network, and all his being
hushed music, poised, alert.

The other prince, unravelled in a swift
plucking of beaks and cruel talons, was
torn into rustling space.

Black sprang from heart of sun.
Full morning bulged. The glare
faded the garden's delicate-spun
filaments. Landscape lay bare.

'A present, for *my* birthday?'
(numbly). He huddled, close
to the summer grass's bouquet
with its little hidden flowers,

and sighed, and stood. And there,
yes, gold & ivory — coming,
clear as before,
shy, his arms half hiding

his present (new and neverending
treasure, always undwindling,
never unsurprising).

From branch sundrench horizon
surging and faintly singing
musics awaken.